An Elegy for Old Terrors

An Elegy for Old Terrors

Poems by Zoé Orfanos

Cover Photograph by Zoé Orfanos
Cover Design by Carla Mavaddat
Text Design by Sonia Tabriz

BleakHouse Publishing
2014

BleakHouse Publishing

Ward Circle Building 254
American University
Washington, DC 20016

NEC Box 67
New England College
Henniker, New Hampshire 03242

www.BleakHousePublishing.com

Robert Johnson – Editor & Publisher
Sonia Tabriz - Managing Editor
Liz Calka - Art Director

Rachel Cupelo - Marketing Director
Shirin Karimi - Senior Creative Consultant
Carla Mavaddat - Curator

Joanna Heaney – Chief Operating Officer
Alexa Marie Kelly – Chief Editorial Officer
Nora Kirk – Chief Development Officer
Rachel Ternes – Chief Creative Officer

Copyright © 2014 by Zoé Orfanos

All rights reserved. No part of this book shall be reproduced or transmitted in any form or by any means, electronic, mechanical, magnetic, photographic including photocopying, recording or by any information storage and retrieval system, without prior written permission of the publisher. No patent liability is assumed with respect to the use of the information contained herein. Although every precaution has been taken in the preparation of this book, the publisher and author assume no responsibility for errors or omissions. Neither is any liability assumed for damages resulting from the use of the information contained herein.

ISBN-13: 978-0-9837769-7-0

Printed in the United States of America

To Vivian and Jeanne—

Two of wisest and wittiest women I have had the pleasure to know. Thank you for being my guiding lights.

Table of Contents

Acknowledgments

I.
Other --- 2
Daylight Savings --- 3
Walking Home After a Storm --- 4
An Elegy for Old Terrors --- 5
Carcass on the Counter: A Holiday Sketch --- 7
The Art of Dying --- 8
Tea With Gene --- 9
On the 44th floor of Tower Apartments (or, Fairytale) --- 10
Chess --- 11
"Dishes with Oysters, Fruit, and Wine" Oil on Panel --- 12
To Monica --- 13
Dream --- 14

II.
Elsewhere --- 16
The Town of Pines --- 17
Subway Paperback --- 18
Fit for this World --- 19
Squeeze --- 20
Desert --- 21
Ritual --- 22
Fluvanna Correction Center for Women, a Still Life --- 23
Number Line --- 24
Without the Crusts --- 25
District Attorney, A Portrait --- 26
Lash --- 27
Storybook --- 28

About the Author
About the Designers
Other Titles from BleakHouse Publishing
More Praise for *An Elegy for Old Terrors*

Acknowledgments

In the first weeks of 2011, Robert Johnson approached me at an American University reception and asked me to join BleakHouse Publishing. Three remarkable years later, his wisdom and my admiration for him as a professor, a publisher, a writer, and a friend has made this book possible.

I am also honored by the incredible work of the BleakHouse Publishing staff, which turned my manuscript from a possibility into a book. Through the keen and tireless efforts of managing editor, Sonia Tabriz, and the inspired design of both Carla Mavaddat and Liz Calka, my work joins a list of books that were beautifully brought into being.

As for the words themselves, I thank the guidance and inspiration of the Departments of English and Creative Writing at American University. Specifically, I esteem the buoyant mentorship of Adam Tamashasky and David Keplinger—both brilliant writers and energetic professors. Thank you for teaching my words how to walk and talk.

To my loving parents Kim and Janet: thank you for bringing me into such a clever and inspiring family. This book is a testament to the years of support, laughter, and love. I look forward to many years and many poems yet to come.

And to my friend, Tiresias: thank you for showing me that every poet needs an oracle.

I would like to take a moment to acknowledge the previous printings of my work. Throughout my time with BleakHouse Publishing, several of my pieces were fortunate enough to be accepted to both *BleakHouse Review* and *Tacenda Literary Magazine*. In the 2011 edition of *BleakHouse Review*, "Tea with Gene" was originally published. In the 2012 edition of the *Review*, "Dream," "District Attorney, A Portrait," and "Lash" (originally "Victimless") were printed. And in the Spring 2013 edition of *Tacenda Literary Magazine*, "Desert" (originally under the title "Untitled") was first printed.

In addition to my work published with BleakHouse, "Daylight Savings" was published in the Fall 2013 printing of American University's *AmLit Magazine*.

I.

Other

Locked in someone else's diary,
You are ink in a loved one's life.

Clipped from every future photo,
Your skin is a dotted line.

Slid through a tight-lipped smile,
Your name trails a pause,

An allusion to a lost life.
(You are a myth.)

Daylight Savings

I had just painted the fourth nail white
when Muna said, So what happens at two?
To be honest, I'd forgotten. I tried
to recall as I slid the vacant hue

onto the fifth finger, but my mind was
flagging under the weight of foreign words
and rhythms that lodged thick stanzas of gauze
in my ears. But then Hanèn turned to her

and said, It's one o'clock again, and each
Arab girl looked at her cell phone to check
the time. I paused over the second hand
and asked, Is time lost in the Middle East?
With five white fingers, the girl from Iraq
said Yes and played an American band.

Walking Home After a Storm

The houses are slowly blinking off
and cement gives way to slick
cobblestones, shining in broken
patterns beneath my feet.

My shadow crouches low to earth,
fingers tracing the cracks,
sliding, whole, into puddles.

I reach for her, forgetting
that the next block has no light pole,
and the browning light won't follow us
over the tangled stones.

But instead of leaving, she surrounds me,
swallowing the puddles and sharp reaches,
sanding the walls to a soft grey.

She absorbs the blue of my blouse, the pink
of my skin, and wraps herself so gently
around me that I don't feel the release
as she ghosts back toward the road.

An Elegy for Old Terrors

It is 2:00 on a Sunday afternoon
and I am awake enough
to wrestle with the white sheets
that constrict around me
and squeeze me into the light
that dryly drenches my bed.

Today I am training to be a clerk
for the primary elections that will be held
on the first Tuesday in May 2011.
I get in the passenger's seat
of my mother's Honda Accord
and we drive downtown arriving
at the courthouse just before four.
Almost all of the doors are locked,
but we find the one open door
and the one sleepy security guard
who is probably working overtime
just to tell us
to take the elevator up to the courtroom
on the fourth floor.

About fifty people file into the room
for the last training session held by the state
for those who want to be clerks and judges.
My mother and I are given two
differently colored folders
because she is a judge
and I am a clerk
and as I hold my folder I stare at the lady
projected two-and-a-half times her size
on the screen in front of us.
As I sit in the repurposed courtroom, I decide
that I would not know this woman
if she were two-and-a-half times smaller
and sitting on the same long, cold bench.

My father meets us outside
and drives my mother's Accord a few blocks
to St. Elmo's Steakhouse
to celebrate the end of my first year of college
and because he has a gift card.
At 6:30 we are seated and quickly served
some of the prettiest and smallest food

that I have ever seen. Across the street
I watch a horse lead a carriage
past the Steak 'n Shake as I take the last bite
of my also tiny strawberry cheesecake.

In a few hours it is late enough
for my parents to say goodnight
and we're so glad that you're home
before my little lamp
with three miniature drawers
is the only source of light
in my quietly familiar house. And as I sit up
in bed with the book that my father leant me,
my phone vibrates with the message
that travelled five hundred and eighty four miles
to ask me if I am watching TV. Suddenly
I am downstairs sitting on the maroon-black
carpeting and staring at the TV as my phone
lights up with more of my roommates' words
AMERICA KILLED OSAMA BIN LADEN
and at almost 2:00 AM I hug my knees
to my chest and wonder how much longer
the crowd of screaming students
played on a loop
will make me sit on the floor
until I can go to bed.

Carcass on the Counter:
A Holiday Sketch

A cream-colored carcass
lolls, wrapped too tightly
in puckered raw sheets
of flesh which cling blueish
to the bones.

Removing the heart,
I strike a match
and watch the body steep
in sweat, as spices stain
the browning carcass.

I slice the tension,
kiss the skin
with a serrated knife
that lingers
in a hot hiss of air.

Shaved and hollow,
the ribs clutch
nakedly
on a doily limp
with grease.

The Art of Dying

"And there were others that did not go anywhere and simply died slower." —Ernest Gaines

He had mastered the art of dying,
of leaving his eleven-year-old Chevy
among the slick, blossoms of oil;
of letting the black blooms grow,
sealing the veins in the crumbling road.

He had mastered the art of dying,
of losing his name to the loud machines
as he repeated it to the foreman;
of remembering the decades of words
he would find if he wrenched back the metal.

He had mastered the art of dying,
of following the sun to his house,
now faded into evening grays,
and thinking a prayer to a probable God
waiting, silent, in the kitchen.

Tea with Gene

I spent each Sunday on a folding chair
by his bed, taking sips of the sun,
surrounded by the framed faces
of those who could no longer take tea.

He called honey "Sunshine in a Bottle."
Can't you see the liquid life? he'd ask,
through the clouds hanging above our tea.
He said he could feel it spreading
every time he took a drink.

What are you doing? he asked between cups.
I showed him a list—a field of slashed words
and fresh ink. He found his name.
He asked again.
"I am here," I said, "drinking tea."

On the 44th floor of Tower Apartments (or, Fairytale)

A blood sun illuminates braided plaits,
trailing the pacing girl. Eyes trained
on the doorknob, her braids coil,
slithering across the pools of red
light, draining from the floor.

The door opens: a man squints
into dying light. The tarnished epaulets
on his jacket match the word stitched
onto the breast: doorman.

Her eyes find him kneeling between coils, countless
men, countless shadows concealing a prince.
Please. Breath escapes through his words.
Let down your hair. Below the horizon,
the sun seals itself.

Chess

Nestling her chin into the maroon carpet,
she wiggles her feet back and forth in the air
as her dress, swishy pink, bunches by her knees.
Eye-level with the checkered board,
she wonders why the little wooden horse
looks nothing like the knights who fight dragons
and search for princesses in pink silk.

Her father sits erect, stories above the world
of faceless little people, each waiting
for him to play them forward.

Head tilted, she rests her cheek on the floor,
and watches the dark horse slide slowly forward
between her father's sideways fingers,
pinched.

"Dishes with Oysters, Fruit, and Wine"
Oil on Panel

Sound stills, the ground drops
And the walls suspend you in four corners.
The gallery is black.
A banquet glows softly, burning
In whites that swirl into oysters
And rake through naked shells.
Slick browns pulse and gleam
In a shade too dim to grant reprieve
From gnarled alien shapes.
A ghost of glass melts into points
Of light, painted softly in the dark.
The liquid captures a window
Too far away to lend light,
A window onto the world
From which this feast came, dredged
By the hand which, stroke-by-stroke,
Presented each dish
For consumption.

To Monica

"Then he descended, a smile on his lips, and murmuring that last word of human philosophy, 'Perhaps!'"
—*Alexandre Dumas*

It took two iced teas to tell
how she wandered in and out of jobs
and cities, pausing long enough to describe
a warm moment with a man, a moment she carries
so closely, that his eyes still reflect in hers.

In my eyes she sees cities, and instead of my tale
she asks for a moment in my head. So I give her a bridge,
rattling with locks, straddling the banks of Paris.
And I build the boulevard, winding along the river.
And so I tell her my tale in moments and in cathedrals.

She fingers a stack of napkins and we write.
"What if, Zoé, what if?"
Bent over the café tables, we write and rewrite
our brittle, brown drafts. I watch as her pen
muddies the paper, writing worried lines
onto the face of a girl on a dirt-packed, Cambodian street.

My own pen begins to sweep through cities,
spreading countries across the countertop,
taking time to speak into each of the napkin's corners.

I revise the Louvre for the fourth time.
We take turns, pronouncing each word, and walking across
the maps of brown paper. My pen hovers

Dream

I was a murderer.
I sat in a scratched, silver chair.
A heavy screen squatted close by.

I watched myself speak.
My skin was stretched across the monitor.
Neither of us flinched.

My eyes and nose and mouth conspired.
They made her grey alien face.
And though I didn't know her answers

I recognized my voice.

II.

Elsewhere

Pace my six by nine and
trip
forty five miles of skyline, hugging
the coast so close you can taste
the salt water
trip
over sandy asphalt in an old sedan full
of giggling faces, flashing camera bulbs,
and sun-slick arms
trip
to the edge of the dunes, feet first
in the sand, toes catching long weeds
as you slide toward the sea
trip
into the surf, smashing white on the shore,
grabbing sand and ankles, pulling
you from the shore, erasing
the faces, muting
the giggles, and ripping
you from the
trip

The Town of Pines

A Cadillac smokes on a rural highway.
The driver's brown curls, sketched
in newsprint, drift below the three clear
faces of her passengers.

With her back to the couch, a mother teases
her daughter's hair into tiny braids.
Both figures glow in the light of nightly news,
Mommy, isn't that Daddy?

Sirens pierce the bank's doors, as a cot creaks
past a locked vault. Uniforms muddle
in flashing lights, collecting the hectic pieces
of the state's single capital case.

She ladled broth into bowls, curls wrestled
under a hair net, scanning the orange line
to spot his smile. On the day of his release,
the pot boiled beneath her blushes.

Subway Paperback

Through grease-black
tunnels, the train
slides,
        a girl leans
into her altered face
in the pane, uneasy,
over the cracked
spine,
        her head tilted
toward fiction
on plastic seats,
the train jolts,
a severed hand slips
into her purse,
              unseen,
a strangled voice leaks
from the speaker,
doors hiss, the chapter
shuts,
        and in the silence
of the streetlight, she searches.

Fit for this World

"You are not fit for this world." —Scott Sundby,
A Life and Death Decision

From the moment you roll back the sheets,
sunlight fills the spaces you leave.
Adjust your jacket over a too-big shirt,
and slide on shoes that rub skin into bone,
as a soapy sink cradles your coffee mug.

Once outside, cling to the sidewalk
as well-tailored forms edge you
from the concrete. Pass between the sun
and the ground as the sidewalk shivers
beneath your shadow.

Your foot slips. The curb shaves the leather
from your shoe, carving up the rubber sole;
take both off, keep walking; the sun slides
down your shoulders, burning away the edges.

Squeeze

my skin squeezes my bones
—constricting softly—
sealing off the pounding
of my life behind a cage
of knifed ribs;

my head rolls back
—rigid—against the noose
of skin around my neck,
carefully contoured
to be airtight.

underneath the stain
of flesh and sticky
murmur of blood,
bones stand bleached
in silent lines, never white
while I'm alive.

Desert

*"You deserve to die."—Scott Sundby,
A Life and Death Decision*

Without any hesitation
she opens the door,
knotted skin on smooth brass,
turning the knob gently.
She ushers in his ragged frame
and he counts excuses
on the table, turning over
his words slowly, each catching
the light like a knife.

Without dissention,
twelve mouths shape
a perfectly rounded yes.
They borrow his words,
leaden gaze on the floor,
you deserve to die.

Ritual

Shamed words shuffle across the lenses
on his face, staining your father's fingers.
Four murderers made today's front page,
claiming countless headlines.

As he finishes his morning ritual,
you are clasped in those tainted fingertips,
wondering how many dead cells
are necessary to cleanse his grayish skin.

Between bites of French toast, he stirs
his coffee—no cream, no sugar—and runs
through lines of bodies. A paragraph
after the freshest funeral, he is late.

Fluvanna Correction Center for Women, a Still Life

A page turns in harmony with a distant buzzer,
as the light marks one more tick on the wall.

In a world *filled with tigers and crocodiles*,
a woman muffles a cough with her fist.

Her nails sink into the cracked spine,
as the sun empties the room in retreat.

She reads until the page dissolves
—*the sea is the cemetery*—in inky black.

Italicized words are from Alexandre Dumas' *The Count of Monte Cristo*

Number Line

At age four he studies the floorboards,
Wood worries the side of cheek,
And under a ceiling of bed springs
He waits for monsters

At age nine he cannot stop climbing,
Until bark scrapes his skin red
And the ground shrinks, consuming
Blades of grass and broken bottles

At age fifteen he learns silence,
And appreciates the calm
Of a small body cooling
In his merciful palms

At age twenty he paces
—An edgy back-alley god
Collecting scars and proof
Of life beneath him

At age twenty-six he is over,
A number and a hollow face
Under a concrete ceiling
Waiting

Without the Crusts

The killer cuts his ham sandwich,
Carving off the crusts,
Because nobody likes the crusts,
And because he would rather take
The time to lay out and slice away
The offending portions
Than be on time for work.

His coworker forgot her lunch
After packing four others, and sits
Imagining four lunch boxes
And four crustless sandwiches
Leaking strawberry preserves
Onto grey plastic tables
Already slick with potato chip grease;

Miles away, a boy sits at his desk
Licking red jam from his fingers
While a substitute teacher
Rakes through the desk
Of a woman who said
She would rather die
Than miss a day of work.

District Attorney, A Portrait

Papers shuffle against an iron-grey suit
as he places the pencil to his mouth.

His teeth find the notches and fill the grooves
as he reaches for another file.

You ask him why he uses pencil.
He smiles. *I don't like stains.*

Opening another manila-colored case,
your name emerges from the graphite smudge

beneath his thumb. A smudge that matches
the small mark left on his temple as he places
the riddled pencil behind his ear.

Lash

Hovering over her coffee, her face
is blurred by clouds.

At the sink, her mother scours
the coffee pot, black

tears seeping from the grounds.
By the stove

her daughter's braids spin the walls
together, lash

at the air.

Storybook

This book's a story
of my absence.
Each page is bound,
There's no table of contents.

Hard-backed, it comes,
standard-issue jacket,
open me up,
find out if I can hack it

in a world where lines
are turned on their sides,
a censored translation
of blood and ink, dried

on the page, snapped clean
by each break, shot through
with a period,
a paragraph of dull ache;

and each chapter reads
much the same as the last,
blow through a few commas,
three more years passed

in a world with no pictures,
just the plain black and white
of a text with no colors,
all the breath I can write.

About the Author

ZOÉ ORFANOS is in her last year as an Honors undergraduate at American University in Washington D.C, after spending a year studying Literature and International Human Rights at Oxford University. Working toward a Bachelors degree in Law and Society with minors in Creative Writing and Literature, Orfanos graduates in May of 2014 from the School of Public Affairs. Orfanos has achieved both Best Short Story and Best Poem for her contributions to The BleakHouse Review. Orfanos served as the 2012 Editor-in-Chief of Tacenda Literary Magazine. Throughout her education, Orfanos has dedicated both time and energy to studying and experiencing the realities of social justice. Having recently volunteered and interned at Offender Aid & Restoration in Arlington, Virginia, Orfanos is now volunteering as a poetry teacher in the Montgomery County Correctional Facility in Maryland.

About the Designers

CARLA MAVADDAT is an undergraduate student majoring in Political Science at McGill University with a passion for photography and design. Mavaddat is interested in human rights and social justice, and tries to incorporate that in her work. Her photos have appeared in Adore Noir, among other venues. She is the Graphics and Design Editor for BleakHouse Review, Art Curator for BleakHouse Publishing, and a Victor Hassine Memorial Fellow.

SONIA TABRIZ graduated from American University (2010) *summa cum laude* with University Honors, with a B.A. in Law and Society and a B.A. in Psychology. She received the Outstanding Scholarship at the Undergraduate Level award for her award-winning works of fiction, legal commentaries, artwork, presentations, university-wide accolades, and academic achievement. Tabriz graduated with a J.D. from The George Washington University Law School, where she served as a Writing Fellow and Editor-in-Chief of the *Public Contract Law Journal*. Tabriz is the Managing Editor of BleakHouse Publishing and designs the text for various publications.

Other Titles from BleakHouse Publishing

Up the River, Chandra Bozelko

Distant Thunder, Charles Huckelbury

Enclosures: Reflections from the Prison Cell and the Hospital Bed, Shirin Karimi

A Zoo Near You, Robert Johnson et al.

Origami Heart: Poems by a Woman Doing Life, Erin George

Tales from the Purple Penguin, Charles Huckelbury

Burnt Offerings, Robert Johnson

More Praise for
An Elegy for Old Terrors

Zoé Orfanos opens her collection, *An Elegy for Old Terrors*, with "Other," a poem that encapsulates our individual lives in eight regnant lines . . . and then continues along a vividly empathetic path that demonstrates a remarkable grasp of the human condition. Each uncomplicated setting shifts seamlessly into an intricate empiricism, as in "Walking Home After A Storm," in which the speaker's shadow "crouches low to earth," evading her grasp until finally "ghosting back toward the road." Or "The Game," in which a young girl watches a chess game while creating a private, hidden world of knights and princesses.

Perhaps even more arresting is the inclusion of poems in Part II that describe and define life, not as the poet has experienced it but as conjured by her imagination and thoughtful examination of other terrors, as in "Elsewhere" and "Number Line." Her masterful invocation of either reality is especially impressive in so young an artist.

Ms. Orfanos has chosen an appropriate title for her book. It is indeed an elegy, one that, in lush, sensual tones, bids farewell to old terrors through a recherché embrace of the world one encounters. It is also a vade mecum that will call to the reader often and should be kept close at hand to save time searching the bookshelves.

- Charles Huckelbury, award-winning poet and author of *Tales from the Purple Penguin* and *Distant Thunder*

www.ingramcontent.com/pod-product-compliance
Lightning Source LLC
Chambersburg PA
CBHW050608300426
44112CB00013B/2128